MOHAMED SALAH
The Egyptian King

A special thank you to Yonatan, Yaron and Guy Ginsberg for their contribution to this book. Their love and depth of knowledge of the beautiful game were invaluable.

Cover photos © front: Brad Penner- Usa Today Sports
back: Reuters/Phil Noble

Cover design and inside page layout: Lazar Kackarovski

Proof editor: Louisa Jordan

Library of Congress Cataloging-in-Publication data available.

U.S. edition

ISBN : 978-1-938591-65-5

eBook ISBN: 978-1-938591-66-2

Published by Sole Books, Beverly Hills, California.

Printed in the United States of America

www.solebooks.com

Mohamed Salah The Egyptian King

Michael Part & Kevin Ashby

More in the Soccer Stars Series:

The Flea – The Amazing Story of Leo Messi

Cristiano Ronaldo - The Rise of a Winner

Neymar The Wizard

James – The Incredible Number 10

Balotelli – The Untold Story

Luis Suarez – A Striker's Story

Thomas Muller – The Smiling Champion

Harry Kane - The Hurricane

www.solebooks.com

The Dark Tunnel

Mo Salah jumped up and down in the tunnel beneath Kiev's Olympic Stadium. The roar of the crowd outside was so loud that his fellow Liverpool striker Sadio Mané had to shout to make himself heard.

"I can't believe we're here. It's the best day of my life!"

Mo grinned back, eyes shining and focused. It was the biggest game any of manager Jurgen Klopp's young team had ever played.

As the match officials at the head of the line started forward, Roberto Firminio turned and gave everyone a thumbs up.

Mo glanced to his left. The Real Madrid players looked as intensely focused as his teammates. Most had played in the Champions League winning teams of the last two years.

But not against us! Mo thought.

The noise when he came out onto the pitch hit him like a tidal wave. The stands heaved with red Liverpool flags and shirts. "You'll Never Walk Alone," Liverpool's anthem, rang excitedly above the drums and trumpets of the Real fans. The Kop, the seats behind the goal, overflowed with standing fans.

Far away, in Mo's home village of Nagrig in Egypt, Mo's family and neighbors packed into a simple concrete block café. A big TV screen took up one end of it. Cheers erupted when Mo's face appeared.

"Yalla, Salah! Yalla, Liverpool!" someone shouted. "Come on, Salah! Come on, Liverpool!"

Mo was Nagrig's and Egypt's hero. His face was painted on the wall of the soccer court outside the café and on murals everywhere. His money had paid for the all-weather pitch that the village youngsters now played on. The only patch of green amongst streets and squares of bright brown dirt. It was just one of the ways he helped everyone.

"Yalla, my son!" Mo's dad, Salah Ghaly, yelled, louder than anyone. It made him so proud seeing his eldest boy up there, running to and fro on the right wing while the teams waited for the kick-off.

"Liverpool will win!" Mo's cousin Abadah shouted. "With Salah and Mané and Firminio, they can't fail."

"In'sh Allah!" Ghaly murmured. "God willing."

To be humble. That had always been his mantra with his quiet, brilliant, single-minded son.

The whistle blew, and cheers went up in the café, in homes across Egypt and the world, and in Kiev.

For twenty minutes, Liverpool had all the play. Mo was everywhere. He got two or three shots on goal, pinged in a dangerous corner, probed and passed, and almost finished Liverpool's best chance. The café roared with his every touch. In Kiev, the first chants began.

"He's the Egyptian King!"

He chased a ball down the center of the pitch, halfway to Real Madrid's goal, jostling with the captain, Ramos. They cartwheeled to the ground. The camera followed the ball as it cannoned away upfield.

Mo knew something was wrong even as he fell.

His right arm, caught in Ramos's, pulled much too far. There was a pop, and a sudden searing pain flooded his right shoulder. He couldn't get up. The camera found him sprawled on his back, surrounded by teammates, calling urgently for the team doctor. The fans went silent. In Nagrig, two hundred men began shouting in despair.

"The shoulder!" Mo gasped as the medical squad sped up to him. He was sitting up now. The only thing in his mind was that they had to fix him, so he could keep playing. He cried in pain as they treated his arm.

"Spray it!" he shouted. "I have to carry on." He stood shakily.

Abadah bellowed into Salah Ghaly's ears. "He's strong! He'll make it!"

Mo's dad nodded nervously. He didn't feel good about the injury at all.

He was right.

Mo began jogging, wincing as he went. For a couple of minutes, he tried to run. But it was no use. He could hardly move his arm without fresh waves of pain. He couldn't challenge, spin, surge, anything. He couldn't play.

Aghast, he sank to the pitch. Tears ran down his face.

It wasn't just this match. Leaving the Champions League final was bad but in only five weeks, the World Cup would begin. His goals and leadership had brought Egypt to the finals for the first time in thirty years. The whole country was bursting with joy and unity at the prospect. It was everything he played for. Bring happiness to his beloved people by showing his game. Now everything was in tatters.

For a moment, it all went dark before his eyes. The pain was everything. He heard the medics explaining he must leave the pitch. He wanted to resist. Tell them, no, I can do it, I can pull through, but all they saw was his lips moving.

A blanket went around his shoulders. He got up mechanically. He saw through the daze Jurgen Klopp's pained face uttering words of comfort and encouragement. He shut his eyes as he disappeared into the tunnel, crushed and in despair.

"Oh, my son," Salah Ghaly moaned. More than anyone, he knew how Mo would be hurting inside. He stood and shouldered his way out into the twilight, texting instantly.

"God will give you strength to recover, my son. Your family is with you. The entire village is with you. All of Egypt is with you."

CHAPTER ONE

The First Game

"Come on, Ab," five-year-old Mo Salah yelled impatiently.

He was hurtling through a forest of legs, occasional slow-moving bicycles, and people coming home from the market or mosque. A ball made of his shirt stuffed with socks stuck to his left foot like glue.

Abadah puffed in the humid shade of the packed dirt street, giggling when Mo made the shirt balloon off a parked van that almost blocked the way.

If *he* tried that, the tightly knotted sleeves would fall undone and they would have to tie it up all over again.

But Mo was amazing. Whatever got in their way, he could lob the makeshift ball, scamper by, and catch the rebound on his instep or knee, like it was on a rubber-band.

Usually after school, they would be knocking the ball back and forth for hours.

Today was different.

Mo's dad had promised to take him to his uncle's café to watch an English Premier League match. It was an early birthday present. The first time he'd go out and watch with all the men of the village. It was Liverpool against Arsenal on Wednesday, May 6, 1998.

And he couldn't wait.

Above him, houses rose in an unbroken line, their balconies so close they nearly touched across the street.

When he got home, the smell of his favorite meal wafted out of the open front door. Fried chicken, fresh greens, and soup. He ran upstairs. His dad sat reading a newspaper on the balcony. In front of him on the floor were a couple of bags of jasmine flowers. His dad sold them, as well as working for the government.

They were all there. Mo's little brother Nasr, his mom, and his two sisters. The table was covered with great dishes. On a silver-scrolled plate was a big round of kanafeh—vermicelli cake soused in syrup and filled with clotted cream. It was Mo's favorite dessert.

"Happy birthday!" everyone chimed in.

He sat down and began to eat hungrily.

"Don't gobble!" his mom scolded. "If you bolt down your food like this every time you go to a game, I won't let you go."

Mo looked up in alarm. His mom's face was solemn, but there was a twinkle in her eye.

"Sorry," he said, and took the next spoonful at a snail's pace.

"It's going to be fun," his dad said from behind his newspaper. "After you've eaten, wash up and change clothes."

"Yes, Dad," Mo said, taking another slow spoonful.

The street was dark by the time Mo and his dad went out of the house. It was quiet on the way to the café. Occasionally, they passed groups of men standing outside doorways, smoking and arguing about the country's leaders. Loud music floated out of some of the balconies. It felt grown-up, a different world. Mo held his dad's hand tightly.

Uncle's café shone brightly next to the youth center soccer court. The hubbub of excited voices poured out of it. When they reached the door, the first thing Mo noticed was the big TV screen filling most of the back wall. Two men in suits talked on it, over a desk with the Premier League logo. The sound was turned low.

"Salah! Mo!" Uncle shouted from behind the counter, where he was serving coffee, mint tea, and sweetmeats. "Right here!"

He waved at a table in front of the TV and they sat down.

Just then, the scene on the TV changed to live coverage from Anfield. The Liverpool players were lined up with the match officials, clapping as the Arsenal team ran out. Uncle turned the sound on. A cheer went up from the crowded café. Mo's hairs stood on end as he heard the Kop singing "You'll Never Walk Alone" as if they were all one voice.

It was twenty-eight minutes before the scoring began. Then, the ball crossed low to Paul Ince on the edge of the box, and his instinctive first touch powered through a forest of legs into the bottom left of Arsenal's goal. Two minutes later, Ince got a second—finishing off a bobbling rebound. Two-nil to the Reds. Mo bubbled with the excitement.

The third goal had him screaming.

McManaman lofted a corner from the left. Ince headed it down toward Michael Owen on the right-hand edge of the box. The eighteen-year-old wonder child's back was to the goal. The ball came at chest height. *Surely all he can do is lay it off,* Mo thought.

No.

Owen leapt off the ground and twisted, bringing his right leg right up and round. The ball flew through the air, straight between the right-hand post and a flailing Alex Manninger, in goal for Arsenal. As the Kop exploded, Manninger sat under the posts, shaking his head.

"Genius!" Uncle shouted.

The entire café exploded with cheers. Mo felt the air filling his lungs. He joined with a scream and he jumped up and down waiving his hands. There was the wonderful skill of a young player on the pitch. The explosion of joy of the crowd cheering in the stadium. All the people who were cheering in the café.

One player brought so much happiness to so many people.

That is special, Mo thought.

"Incredible!" His dad shouted in his ears, smiling.

Mo had never seen his dad so excited.

"It's the most amazing birthday gift!" Mo said, his eyes sparkling. "Thank you, Daddy!"

He would remember this moment many years later. On that night, Mo could think of nothing except that leap, twist, and unerring shot of Michael Owen.

When he pictured the shot, all he wanted was to be that player. He felt that was what he wanted to do. That was what he wanted to be. He would do anything to play in front of that crowd and score amazing goals and then run toward the stands and smile at the cheering fans.

And with this picture in mind, he fell asleep. When his mom came into the room, she found him deep in sleep, a smile on his lips, gripping the ball made out of socks.

CHAPTER TWO
Street Genius

"I want to play in the Premier League," Mo said, as he hurried toward the youth center soccer court with his friends. They were still too young to play for Nagrig Juniors, but they wanted to kickabout where the older kids played. "I will play for Liverpool one day," he added.

Abadah and Mohammed laughed. "Mo, it's impossible. No-one from Nagrig gets a chance like that," Abadah said.

Mo dinked the ball ahead and raced off, the others in hot pursuit. "I will," he said.

The soccer court had walls all around, but there was a hole you could get through. The pitch was dirt and strewn with litter and the walls were covered in murals, but Mo thought of it as his kingdom. He curled the stuffed shirt through the gap and scrambled after.

Five older boys were already there playing. They glanced toward him. Mo recognized them as in their last year of basic school. They had the Nagrig youth kit on, and a real soccer ball. It was battered and frayed, but still a real ball.

"Play you," Mo challenged impulsively, eyes fixed hungrily on the ball.

The boys didn't bother answering. Mo stepped up to them. He so wanted to kick that ball.

"Afraid I'll beat you?" Mo said, brightly. "I'll give you a goal head start."

He smiled. The biggest boy faced him, frowned a moment, then unexpectedly nodded.

"I've seen you on the school pitch," he said. "We'll give you a game. But first you have to get the ball."

Mo was fearless. On the school playground, no-one could get the ball off him. He winked at his friends, dropped the stuffed shirt expertly onto his left knee, and sent it unerringly into the top right corner of the rusting goalposts. The big boy kicked the real ball the other way and ran down the pitch. Mo sprang after him.

For a moment, it looked as if Mo would be beaten, but soon he scampered level and swung with all his might. The ball pinged off his bare foot like a rocket and ricocheted off the side wall of the court. Mo's toes stung, but the ball came straight back to him. In a blur, without thinking, he controlled it with his instep and took off.

The ball felt like a live animal, the way it bounded ahead. Mo had to use all his speed to keep possession. But it felt natural.

He steered instinctively away from the rest of the older boys, found an angle, and shot.

One-nil to the seven-year old.

For an hour, Mo single-handedly kept the five older boys honest. Abadah and Mohammed huffed and puffed and supported and once in a while passed or sent the ball toward the goal. Suddenly, the biggest boy stopped playing and picked up the ball, looking nervously toward the soccer pitch gate.

"Don't stop!" Mo shouted.

He turned around. Mr. Ghamri el-Saadani was standing there. Mr. el-Saadani coached the Nagrig youth center team. His dad knew him. They played together when Mo's dad was a young kid. The older boys ran and lined up in front of him. Mr. el-Saadani acknowledged them, but he was really looking in Mo's direction.

"We'll have to go," Abadah said, coming up.

Feeling Mr. el-Saadani's eye, Mo turned red and scampered off.

CHAPTER THREE

Nagrig Juniors

A knock came on the front door.

"Ghamri!" Mo heard his dad say. "Come in. Have some coffee and kanafeh."

The Nagrig Juniors youth coach hadn't come on a social visit. When everything was cleared away and he sat on the balcony, he glanced at Mo and then addressed his dad quietly.

"Mo was on the Juniors' pitch again today. I tell you Salah, he's fast. Better than we ever were."

Mo's dad laughed and then frowned in Mo's direction before turning back.

"I don't know what to do with him, Ghamri. Mo's a quiet, respectful boy. A good boy. But he can't think of anything but soccer. His school reports get worse and worse. He doesn't concentrate."

The coach nodded. "I was thinking. Perhaps … if Mo's soccer was more focused … if he came to the youth center for some proper training when the season starts again in August. It might help."

"Mo has to study," his mom said. "He can't play his life away. It can't be soccer, soccer, soccer—or he'll never get a job."

"That's right," his dad said. He turned toward Mo, who had his head down. "I know you're listening, son. What do you have to say?"

The only thing in Mo's head was the feeling of the real ball at his feet. He would do anything to get that again.

"I promise," he said, humbly, "if I begin Juniors early, I'll study extra hard. I'll get better grades."

"You'll come straight home from school?" his mom said, "and do your homework?"

Mo took a deep breath. It would mean giving up kickabout. But if he wanted to play Premier League, he had to start somewhere. He looked up and nodded.

He saw his father exchange a nod with the coach.

Mr. el-Saadani rose from the chair. "Mo, I'll see you tomorrow at four o'clock sharp," he said.

"Yes, sir," Mo said. His body shook with excitement. He wanted to run out and play right now in the middle of the night.

Before he went to bed, his mom came and hugged him. "I'll be a good student," he promised.

"Soccer is nice but only a good education will get you further in life," she said,

He nodded. "When I grow up, I'll get a real job," he said.

She smiled, hugged him, and shut off the lights.

Before he fell asleep, all he thought of was the moment he would step onto the training pitch for his first official practice.

The next day, Mo raced out on the youth center soccer court with two dozen other boys.

"Hey, Mo!" a voice shouted. It was one of the older boys, Boutros, who he had played kick-about against. "You'll have to learn to *pass* the ball now!"

Mo didn't reply. Without his mates and cousins, he felt nervous. He looked round the dilapidated court and a sudden shiver went through him. He had something to prove. He hoped he didn't mess up.

Coach Ghamri el-Saadani called them to attention. They lined up and he looked at them with a stern look.

"OK, boys. Please give me your attention. Quiet please!"

He waited until everyone was silent.

"We all love soccer, don't we?" he continued. "And we all want to be good players?"

Everyone looked at each other. "Yes, sir," one of the boys said and the rest chimed in.

"So, we have to work hard and be focused. We have to listen and learn. We have to help each other. You know why?"

No one answered. The coach continued. "Because soccer is a team game. You live by the team and you die by the team. All the biggest stars in the world wouldn't be successful without their teammates. So, the first thing we'll learn here is to trust your teammates."

Mo was sure he felt Mr. el-Saadani's eyes flick momentarily in his direction.

"Any questions?" the coach asked.

"No, Mr. el-Saadani," the boys chorused.

"Good. We'll start with warm-ups and later will work on passing."

After some running and stretches, the coach put them in a big circle around him. He drilled the ball to each of them in turn and they passed it back to him.

After a while, he stepped away and began calling out names. The boys passed one to another across the circle. It was harder than it looked. When it got to Mo's turn, he was sure the coach called faster.

"One touch next time!" Mr. el-Saadani warned, after Mo brought the ball back with his left, teed it up with his right and sent it straight into Boutros's instep. Mo nodded and concentrated. When the pass came to him again, he moved, looked, and hit it first time. He found he was sweating.

At the end of the session, Mr. el-Saadani shook hands with each of the boys as they filed out through the gate.

"Good," he said to Mo, smiling. "You did well."

Mo's eyes shone with pride. He didn't want to leave the pitch. He wanted it to last forever.

At school, Mo's grades didn't get better, but they stopped getting worse. His parents were pleased.

One evening, Mo plucked up his courage and asked Mr. el-Saadani if someone from Nagrig could ever play for Liverpool.

A kind smile spread over Mr. el-Saadani's face. "Mohamed, there is no end to what you can achieve with talent, determination, focus, and hard work. But we have to accept what God wills for us. The opportunity may not come."

Mo looked up into his face, swallowing hard. "I can work hard." His voice fell to a whisper. "Do I have the talent?"

Mr. el-Saadani smiled. "Of course you have talent, Mohamed. And with hard work, who knows? You could be the hero of Egypt one day."

Mo's heart beat again. "So, I'll work even harder," he said.

He was true to his word. Every day, he would come home from school, do his homework hurriedly, then rush out to practice. He watched soccer whenever he could and he learned a lot. His parents noticed his dedication, and how he really improved his play.

"I was never so focused," his father said one day to his mother. "I loved soccer, but it was just fun. Mo is different. He's so serious about it. When he tells me he wants to be a professional player I hold myself because I don't want to crush his hopes but what chance does he have, coming from here? No one around here ever became a pro."

Mo's mom listened. Everything his dad said rang true. But there was something in Mo's eyes that told her maybe he'll be able to fulfill his dream.

CHAPTER FOUR

El Mahalla City

Mo thrust the iron grill from the thick double doors of his home and jumped onto the quiet early evening street. He'd finished study and was going to knock on Abadah's and Mohammed's doors. He had his number ten Zidane Juventus shirt on. He wanted to play.

"Son! Wait!"

He recognized his dad's shout coming from the top of the road and turned to wave at him, grinning broadly. He stood obediently as his dad came up and put his two hands on Mo's shoulders.

"Eaten yet?"

"Yes," Mo replied, brow creasing in surprise.

His dad nodded, as if happy. "It'll do. Come on. Get in the car."

"But I was going for a pick-up game with friends," Mo protested, his voice trailing off.

"You're going somewhere better than that," his dad smiled, putting on his seatbelt.

"What do you mean?"

His dad only patted his finger on the side of his nose and winked.

They wove through the narrow Nagrig streets past bare fall jasmine fields onto the main road. Mo had no idea where they were headed. His stomach churned with curiosity.

The sun went down. They kept on driving. They joined a motorway where there were more cars than Mo had ever seen in his life.

At last they came to a city with buildings twice the size of any in Nagrig and stopped in front of a stadium with four huge floodlit chimneys behind it.

Crowds of fans wearing light blue jerseys streamed through the stadium turnstiles. Mo could hear drums and the sound of firecrackers and chanting inside.

"Welcome to Ghazl al-Mahalla, Son, or The Farmers," his dad said. "They're playing Al-Ahly tonight."

"An Al-Ahly game?" Mo's mouth was agape. Al-Ahly was one of the two Cairo-based teams who always shared the Egyptian Premier League title between them. Wherever you lived in Egypt, you either supported them or Zamalek, the other title-chasers. Mo and his family cheered for Al-Ahly, the Reds. Abadah was a Zamaleki. It was a constant source of friendly joshing.

His dad nodded. "You deserved a reward for all your hard work."

"Thank you, Dad," Mo hugged his father tight. He was so excited he began jumping up and down. His dad laughed. He knew the feeling. He remembered his first real game.

They found a street trader and bought shawarma for them to eat. Mo ate the lamb and pitta bread sandwiches, dripping with tahina sauce, with relish. Then they filed in with the rest of the fans and took their seats near the center line, in the middle row.

It was Mo's first time at a top-flight match and he drank in everything. The pitch swept to his left and right, so much longer and wider than on TV. When the players ran on, they felt so close you could touch them. And he could hear the ball, when they kicked it. It was awesome.

As for the din of the fans—it was a never-ending mutter, moan, or roar. It reminded Mo of the Egyptian summer wind.

Al-Ahly won at a canter, three goals to one. Mo didn't register much of the game itself, only the excitement. He bounded out of his seat when Al-Ahly scored, groaned when Ghazli got a penalty, and jumped in ecstasy as the keeper parried the spot kick. Afterward, he was spellbound. He couldn't get the joy out of his mind.

When he got home, he sank into bed overflowing with gratitude.

At training next day, Mr. el-Saadani announced the team for Nagrig Juniors first away matches of the season. Mo was excited to find he would be on the bench. They were playing in a tournament robin in Basyoun, against five other teams. Basyoun was ten miles away, and ten times bigger than Nagrig. Teams from there always beat Nagrig.

Mr. el-Saadani, Mo's father, and a couple of other parents drove the team. The air was dry and dusty. On the way out of Nagrig, a line of cows wandering between the jasmine fields blocked the road. Mo almost bounced out of his seat in frustration.

When they arrived, Mr. el-Saadani called the team together.

"Remember. Don't panic if the other team score first. Pass to each other and help each other." He paused and grinned. "And have fun!"

Mo didn't play in the first two games. They went as usual. Nagrig played with heart, but the opposition was too good. They lost one zero in both games.

In the third game, Mr. el-Saadani let Mo in. He passed well and fought for the ball. In the last minute, the teams were tied with no goals.

The ball came to Mo's feet in the middle of the pitch. Straight away, one of the boys from Basyoun was on him. Mo looked around. He could pass back, but the kid in front of him had spread his legs. In a flash, Mo nutmegged him and darted forward. He rounded one defender, then another, and saw the helpless goalkeeper before him. He lashed with his left and the ball was in.

The whistle blew. Nagrig had won the game! The team mobbed Mo from all corners of the pitch. He looked sheepishly at the bench, but even Mr. el-Saadani was smiling.

Mo saw the smiles on his teammates' faces, and the joy he brought to his coach and to his proud dad.

It felt great. He was happy because he made other people happy.

CHAPTER FIVE

"Be humble, Son"

Mo Salah froze, his back to the goal.

"Tackle him, Ab'!" his little brother Nasr shouted.

They were playing after school in the youth center soccer pitch. It was just like before they joined the youth side. No-one had shoes on, and they were using Nasr's stuffed shirt.

Abadah hovered between Mo and the rusty posts. He was head and shoulders taller than Mo now, although both were ten.

Before Ab could poke his foot between Mo's legs, Mo spun, sending the ball to one side and sprinting around the other.

Ab lunged.

It was pointless.

Mo had the ball at his feet in a heartbeat and rifled off a shot with his left, not even breaking stride. It sailed into the top right corner, past a stunned Mohammed Basyouni in goal, bouncing off the wall behind with a clunk.

"Too *slow*, Ab," Mo crowed, setting off on his victory sprint.

In his imagination, the five-story apartment blocks overlooking all sides of the pitch were the stands at the Ghazli stadium. The shirts, pants, and bed linen flapping from the balconies in the scorching Egyptian heat were the scarves and banners. The open windows and baked brown bricks were full with faces, all chanting his name.

"Mo, you are too quick. Give us a *chance*!" Ab moaned.

Mo grabbed the ball and faced them.

"OK. All of you against me. Only you have to get the ball first."

He dropped it onto his left toe and set off. There were eight of them, including Nasr, whose mom had been sent to call Mo in for dinner, and friends and fellows from the youth center.

"Charge!" Basyouni yelled. Basyouni, Ab, and Nasr made for him in a line.

He tipped the ball over their heads, wove through the boys behind them like a slaloming bicycle, and emerged with no-one left between him and goal. He lofted the ball downfield in an unerring goal-bound arc.

"Totti chips the keeper and scores again!" he chirped, mentioning the Italian striker who was one of his favorites.

Nasr zipped past him in a blur, chasing the ball faster than his skinny eight-year-old legs had ever moved. To Mo's disbelief, his little brother actually got there in time, sliding through the dust and toeing the ball off the line just as it dropped out of the sky.

Nasr jumped up, right shin grazed, eyes shining, trying not to wince.

"Saved it!" he triumphed.

Mo laughed good-naturedly. "You did, baby brother. Maybe you'll make it one day too. Although I doubt it."

"Mo!"

A stern voice came from the gate. It was Mr. el-Saadani.

"It's Friday. You should be getting ready for prayers."

Just as he spoke, a tinny wail echoed across town, from the village mosque. It was the call to prayer, sent out on speakers so everyone could know it was time.

Mo felt a sudden pang of guilt.

"See you tomorrow," Mo yelled, as he let the ball fall once again to the ground and dribbled it like lightening through the gate and onto the street.

He washed and changed when he got home. Smells of cooking oil, herb-soup, and falafel filled the air as he walked with all his family along the narrow streets to mosque. When they got to the entrance, his dad stopped him.

"Son," his dad began, "Mr. el-Saadani visited me at work today. Do you know why?"

Mo's heart beat hard, but he shook his head.

"He tells me you're a great asset. You're talented. You listen. You work hard."

Mo looked at the ground in embarrassment but his eyes shone. This was what he wanted. His dad cupped his chin and made him look up at his face. His eyes were grave but loving. "He also told me you're too cocky."

Mo's eyes widened.

"You don't appreciate your teammates the way you should."

"But they make mistakes," Mo mumbled. "They don't score goals like I do. I'm better."

"Son!" his dad said, sternly, "Always be humble. And always be kind to others."

Tears brimmed in Mo's eyes. He nodded mutely.

"Your mom and I are very proud of you," his dad continued, gently. "But don't spoil your hard work with a bad attitude to the people around you."

Mo nodded. "I'll be humble," he said.

CHAPTER SIX

Chances and Doubts

Eleven-year-old Mo yanked open the iron grill in front of the oak door of his house and charged inside.

"Dad, Mom. Pepsi came to school today. They gave out kits. We're going to have a team. The tryouts are next week."

He stood in the hall, yelling to anyone who would listen. Seconds later, cannoning into him, his little brother Nasr bounded off the street with the same story.

His mom came calmly out of the kitchen, her hands covered with flour.

"What are you talking about?"

"*Pepsi,* mom!" Nasr repeated.

"There is a new five-a-side league for school teams," Mo announced, pulling himself together and managing not to throw himself around the room in ecstasy.

"I suppose you want to play in it," his mom replied. She wasn't thrilled.

"I have to," Mo said, determinedly. "The man said ..." Mo paused to remember the words exactly. They were important and he had to make it sound real.

"He said this was a program to help develop skills and provide opportunities for talented young soccer players."

His mom looked unconvinced.

"The government are behind it too," Mo said.

His mom sighed.

"Please, Mom. Everyone wants me to try out. Don't you think it's my chance?"

"Of course you'll try for the team, Mo," she replied, "But why is your head only into soccer. What about school?" She sighed again. "Finish your homework first."

"Yes, Mom," he said and walked to his room.

If only she would understand. Maybe one day she would, he thought, his heart beating hard.

In the evening he told his dad about the new program. "Dad," he said, "why does Mom worry so much? *You* played soccer all the time when you were little. You told me so."

His dad didn't reply straight away. When he did, what he said was unexpected.

"Son, you start middle school in September. If you do well, you'll get into a good high school and go on to university. But if you fail …" He paused. "What do you want to do in your life?"

"I want to play soccer for Egypt. I want to play in the European Leagues. Mr. el-Saadani says, if I work hard, and if God wills ..."

His dad's face clouded.

"Most soccer players are not successful. And after fifteen years, they stop playing. Then what? Nagrig is poor. Egypt is poor. If you're thirty years old and uneducated what chance is there for you? Mom wants you to have a decent job."

Mo thought about it. "It just means I have to be very good," he said after a while. "Like Ronaldo."

Cristiano Ronaldo was Mo's latest obsession. He became an English Premier League player at the age of eighteen. He came from a poor family in Madeira. He was a midfield wizard who was also a goal scorer, like Zidane and Totti.

I bet Ronaldo's dad believed that his son could make it, Mo thought.

His dad put a hand on Mo's shoulder. "Mo—do you think you're that good?"

Mo looked up sharply. "I am humble. Really. Whatever happens is God's will. But ... I'm better than anyone I've played against. Mr. el-Saadani says I'm better than anyone he's ever seen. And ... Ronaldo was a kid like me, right? And his dad believed he could be great!"

Mo's father held his gaze. Mo's voice dropped. "I need to test myself, don't I?"

His dad nodded slowly. "No-one from Egypt has ever become a real world star, Mo."

Mo didn't answer. He wasn't discouraged. In his dreams he already did it.

"Well done, Mo," Mr. el-Saadani said, as the boys filed out of the gate after training. "You worked extra hard today."

Mo stopped and shook his head. He wasn't happy. "The ball doesn't go where I plan, sir."

His coach thought about it. He knew what Mo meant. "That's why we train. Training never stops. Ever," he said. "You get that." He was impressed.

Next day, before breakfast, Mo was back at the soccer court. He put a marker down just inside the rusty posts and paced out onto the pitch. For the next hour, he practiced free-kicks from every part of the pitch, aiming for the marker.

He got better.

With his parents blessing, he joined the Pepsi School's "Dawry Al-Madares" League that year, and his dribbling, his speed, and his scoring skills became known beyond Nagrig. He didn't know it, but he had begun to get a reputation.

CHAPTER SEVEN

Maggi

The day after Mo finished Basic School, Mo's dad announced a challenge.

"You need to play with better players, Son. Mr. el-Saadani knows the coach at Ittihad Basyoun. They've seen you in the Schools League and they want you to train with them. I've agreed."

Ittihad Basyoun, which means Basyoun United, wasn't in the Egyptian Premier League, but still a real soccer club. Mo forced himself not to dance up and down around the breakfast table.

"Thank you so much, Dad," he said trying not to scream in joy.

"Won't be easy," his dad said. "Next Monday is your first training."

"Wait five days?" Mo was disappointed. He was eager to be at training right away.

The first time he went there, he was thrilled. Ittihad's playing pitch was covered with grass. It was full-size, and on every side was a low concrete terrace. At each training session, few men and a bunch of kids stood on the terraces. They were Ittihad fans or relatives of the youth players.

At the end of the first training session, the coaches made everyone take five penalties. Mo remembered the practices he'd put in and banged a couple low to the right, and the rest to the left, making the side-netting bulge. It was precision. Even when the keeper guessed correctly and threw himself as far as possible, the ball beat his outstretched fingers.

After Mo's last kick came the unmistakable sound of clapping on the terraces. Mo couldn't believe his ears. He was a bit embarrassed but if felt good.

Going there was harder than Mo imagined. Twice a week, he had to bike half an hour through deserted fields of cotton and the busy town neighborhood. Being away from his friends felt lonely but it was worth it. He knew that each training session made him a better player.

By the time of the second round of the Pepsi tournament, Mo had impressed the coaches enough to get a place on the A team. All his family drove through a warm winter's day to the tournament venue, an indoor court in Basyoun. For once, a little gray rain sprinkled the fields. Mo sat in front, gazing through the front window, lips moving silently.

"I'm practicing," he said, when his mom leaned forward to ask what he was doing.

"I'm imagining the drills, and executing them perfectly. It gets me in shape."

His mom held his gaze quietly. She was impressed.

He beamed at her.

Mo loved the atmosphere of the indoor venue. It was packed with parents and families and coaches. Every sound was amplified. You could imagine you were playing in front of a real crowd. Mo's family found seats near the touchline and sat down.

"Ghaly?" a man said, just to their left. Mo's dad looked up. Someone from Nagrig.

"Hey, nice to see you. Who are you here for?" he asked the man. A girl sat with him.

"We have a cousin in Mahalla whose son is here. This is my daughter Maggi. She is soccer crazy." The man smiled.

A shy mumbled hello. Mo's dad smiled, cupped their faces in his hand, and introduced his own children.

Midway through the first match, Mo picked up the ball on the halfway line, jinked left, right, then left again. Suddenly, he could see the goal. The keeper was a bit off his line. The five-a-side goal was small, the angle awkward. It would need a pinpoint shot.

His eyes flickered round. Everyone was marked.

Why not?

He swung his left leg.

The ball went like a laser, too fast for the keeper even to move.

It was spectacular.

One-zero to Basyoun.

Mo's face broke into a wide shy smile.

As he jogged back past his parents, he noticed the girl next to them, her face perfectly round in her scarf. She looked at him intently, not clapping or waving her arms, but with eyes shining in encouragement. He felt himself blush.

"Good job, son!" he heard his dad shout. "Go for it, Mo!" he heard from the man next to his family.

He went back to the play with his heart beating fiercely.

In their final match, Basyoun needed to win their last match to progress to the next stage. So did their opponents, a team from Mahalla. It was a tense game, still nil-nil as the second half drew to a close.

The ball bobbled around the penalty area. It came to Mo's feet. The Mahalla keeper dared not let him tee up. He burst off his line and barged Mo away, making no attempt to play the ball. The whistle went for a penalty.

Mo grabbed the ball.

This one was his.

The Basyoun players lining the penalty area were like a guard of honor as Mo ran up to take the kick. He rifled it unerringly into the top of the net. Everyone erupted and charged up to him, even the keeper. From the sidelines, he heard his family yelling with triumph. Even his mom.

He twisted his head and looked in their direction. The girl was looking straight at him again, as rapt and still as before. A smile shone on her face.

On the way home, he couldn't get her out of his head.

Nasr jabbered about the penalty but Mo had a question to ask.

"Mom," he said, suddenly, trying to sound casual. "Who were those people next to you? The ones with a girl?"

"People from our town," his mom said. "Their cousin's son from Mahalla was playing. Her name is Maggi. Very nice girl."

Mo didn't look back at his mom. He just stared ahead blushing.

CHAPTER EIGHT

The Scout from Tanta

As the season drew to an end, more spectators began to gather for the training sessions in Basyoun. Mo got used to being watched by strangers. Sometimes, the watchers talked to the coaches after the session.

The two dozen lads of Basyoun Under-13s were waiting to begin training when the coaches brought someone new to see them. They didn't say who he was, only that he was going to take the session today.

The man wore shiny training gear but Mo couldn't see any team logo on it.

"My name's Mohammed," the man began. "I don't want you to do anything special. Just warm up and play a game."

He got the boys into lines and made them do some loosening exercises, then divided them into teams. He blew his whistle and the game began.

Mo's dad was one of the men on the sideline that night. It was hot. The sun had just set. He turned to the man next to him, a guy who came every week.

"Who's he?" he asked.

"It's a scout," the man whispered. "I've seen him before. He's from Osmason Tanta Sporting Club."

"A Tanta scout?" Salah Ghaly said in amazement. Tanta S.C. were one of the oldest clubs in Egypt. They hovered in and out of the Egyptian Premier League. "Who's he come to see?"

His companion shrugged. "We've more than one excellent prospect this year."

Salah Ghaly turned to watch the kickabout game, hoping his son would perform well.

Everyone was at their peak that night and it pushed Mo to excel himself. He dribbled, passed, sped into space, and scored two fine goals. Salah didn't want to get his own hopes up, but it looked like the stranger paid attention. At the end of the session, he beckoned to Mo and went over to the coach with him. They began talking, and then Mo gestured over to the touchline. They came over toward Salah Ghaly.

The man introduced himself, holding out his hand. "How old is your son?"

"Thirteen next month." His dad tried to stay calm.

The man nodded. "You're happy for your son to give up a lot of time to soccer?"

Salah chuckled. "I'm happy for him to work hard. He's a good boy and not a bad student either."

The man smiled and nodded again.

"That's great. Can you bring him to our club next week? I'd like him to try with our Under-14 youth."

Mo kept his head bowed respectfully.

"If you accept my son," Salah said, slowly, "what are the commitments?"

"Trainings three evenings a week and a match day."

Salah looked at Mo questioningly. Mo looked up, his eyes shining, nodding enthusiastically.

"I'll work doubly hard. I promise."

Salah gave his hand to the man trying hard not to show how excited he was.

Next week, Salah put on his best clothes before driving his son for an hour to reach Tanta city. Tanta was the capital of Gharbia province, a city of broad streets lined with trees and thousand-year-old mosques. Mo's spine tingled as they drove through.

When they reached Tanta Sporting Club's grounds, Mo's eyes popped out. It was a huge complex: tennis courts, swimming pools, a lake for rowing, and a stadium with eight thousand seats. All the grass around was a deep green. Mo had never seen so much in one place.

The people going in and out looked wealthy. Salah Ghaly looked at his son.

"Nice, isn't it?" he said.

Mo nodded.

Inside the training ground, Mo saw the same deep green as the main pitch. The man who invited them was waiting there with an assistant. There were about thirty boys on the pitch already. Most looked a lot bigger and stronger than Mo. Mo took a deep breath and marched over. They all looked nervous. A couple of minutes later, two more boys joined, running onto the pitch.

"Mo Salah," Mo said, smiling and offering his hand to the boy next to him.

"Ibrahim," the boy muttered back. He looked like he was sweating.

The coach clapped once and everyone gave him their attention.

"Boys, some of you know how we train. Some of you are new. But you're all on trial tonight. There are eighteen places on the squad. Do your best."

Mo thought it wasn't the most confidence-boosting speech he'd ever heard, but it didn't matter. He was determined to do well.

They started with passing drills, and moved on to cone work, spot kicks and, at the end, a game. Mo wasn't so happy with the way he performed. He missed a sure goal at the beginning of the game, and although he went on to give some good assists and score from a free-kick, he thought he'd blown it. All the way home, his stomach churned with the fear that he had missed his chance. He threw himself on his bed, imagining that all his dreams were in rags. As the days progressed, he grew more and more gloomy. A week passed.

They're not going to call. They don't want me. I blew it.

That's when the phone rang. Salah Ghaly walked in to the boys' bedroom and gazed at Mo calmly.

"They want you, Mo. Tanta S.C. want you on their Under-14 squad."

Mo sank to his knees in relief. Then he took his ball and ran to the street looking for his friends. He had to play. It was time to celebrate.

CHAPTER NINE

A Letter from Cairo

"Want to play?" Nasr held a ball under his arm.

Mo looked up from the doorstep and grinned. "Sure."

It was a quiet June afternoon. The hot narrow lane was deserted. Nasr took the ball expertly up past the parked bicycles and vans and turned.

"Like when we were little," he enthused.

Mo smiled broadly back, stuffing his letter of acceptance at Basyoun Industrial Secondary School into his back pocket. He gestured his little brother forward.

Nasr caressed the ball with his right foot and then his left, approaching Mo lazily. Mo spread, and when Nasr drew level with him, lunged swiftly forward. Nasr cupped the ball over Mo's outstretched leg and dodged past.

"Great!" Mo said, happily. "You're learning!"

Nasr turned around, squaring the ball up for the return run. "I'll never be as good as you, Mo."

Mo's smile turned wistful. "Am I so good? I don't think so."

Nasr toyed with the ball as he came forward, laughing incredulously. Behind him, at the end of the street, a goat crossed the road.

"Mo, you were the best player in school, the best at Ittihad Basyoun, and now you're the best at Tanta."

He ran forward and tried a nutmeg. This time, Mo was onto the ball in a flash, catching it on his back heel, spinning it delicately, and punting it expertly back through Nasr's legs.

"See?" Nasr said, rooted to the spot.

Mo caught up with the ball and scooped it into his hands.

"It's not enough," he said flatly, turning back toward Nasr and kneeing the ball in his direction. The younger boy controlled it on his instep and lifted it back.

As they kept the ball in the air between them, Mo went on. "I go into High School in the fall. I'll have to choose soon. Unless I can be a pro at a big club, I'll have to concentrate on my studies."

"Doesn't Tanta count?" Nasr asked, breathlessly.

Mo shook his head. "They don't pay well. Not even first-team players."

"But you can't give up!" Nasr protested.

Mo didn't say anything. He knew his brother was right. He wanted more than anything to give his life to soccer. But he was fourteen now and the eldest son. Childhood was coming to an end. The family needed him to do well and get a decent job.

"Mo, watch out, behind you!" Nasr's shout jolted Mo out of his thoughts.

"What?" As Mo tried to turn, he felt something tugging him backward.

It was the goat, its teeth fastening hungrily onto the flapping tail of his number ten jersey.

"Get off, you animal!" he shouted laughing. "It's my favorite!"

As Mo wrestled manfully with the goat, Nasr broke down into gales of laughter.

"We have something important to talk about," his dad said one evening. He held a letter in his hand. "Have a seat." The sweet smell of drying jasmine leaves floated round the room. His mom smiled thoughtfully at Mo as he sat down.

Mo knew it was important. He saw his dad trying to control his emotions.

He held the letter out to him. "Look at this."

Mo frowned. He started to read, then stopped and blinked. Was this a joke?

At the top of the page was a blue and yellow shield with soccer players, swimmers, and rowers inside it. The address next to it was familiar.

Mo stared at it. It couldn't be.

"The Arab Contractors Sports Club scouts have been watching you," his dad said.

"They want you to join their youth academy," his mom continued, as if that were the most normal thing in the world.

Mo felt tears springing to his eyes. He dashed them away. *Arab Contractors—El Mokawloon? The Egyptian Premier League team? From Cairo? They wanted to train him?*

"If we agree to it, son, you will have to work harder than you ever imagined," his dad began. "It's a four-hour journey, each way, day after day."

Mo broke into his dad's sentence with a trembling voice. "You're *thinking* of letting me go?!"

"It would be up to you to make it work," his mom said, her voice warm. "You would have to work hard in school and in training."

Mo's gaze swung incredulously from one parent to the other, as if he was watching a tennis game.

Then he shouted uncontrollably: "I'll never take it easy. I promise!"

His mom smiled, wiping a tear from her eyes. His father looked at his son with an appraising stare and hugged him.

"Yes, my son."

"You agree?"

"Let's try it for a month. See if you can handle it."

Mo smiled. He was sure he could handle it. He began leaping round the room and whooping with joy. His parents laughed. They too were overjoyed. And then he left home.

"Where is he going?" his dad wondered.

His mom smiled. She knew that Mo had become good friends with Maggi, the girl who watched him play in the tournament for Basyoun. In the years since they'd met at the youth match, they'd become good friends.

His mom was right. When Mo arrived at her house, Maggi saw him smiling. She smiled back.

"Good news?" she asked.

"Yes," he said, his heart filled with pride.

CHAPTER TEN

First Day at Mountain Wolves

Mo's dad drove for three hours and there was still another hour to go. Mo had never been so far from home. His excitement and nerves had been building ever since they left, just after breakfast.

His dad talked the whole time. "When your coach speaks to you, listen, Son. Be respectful."

Mo nodded. "Yes, Dad."

"What's your coach's name?"

"Handi Noor."

"What will *you* call him?"

"Sir."

"I will be watching you, Son."

Mo smiled. The coach's name made his heart thump. *Handi Noor* would teach him! The man had played for *Egypt!*

"Tell me again the names of the buses."

When he did this journey alone, it would be by bus. Blinking, Mo went through the list.

His dad lapsed into silence and Mo gazed once again at the endless fields of cotton and ripening greens.

Suddenly, on the very far horizon, he saw the glittering summits of skyscrapers, like a forest of light.

Cairo.

His heart leapt inside him.

It was huge. Mile after mile of homes, factories, shops, and towering buildings. It seemed they had been driving through them forever. How his dad knew which way to turn was a mystery. Mo's stomach wound tighter and tighter, wondering would they ever arrive?

All at once, Osman Ahmed Osman complex, El Mokawloon's Nasr City base in Cairo, loomed out of the nest of narrow streets. They drew up to the main entrance amongst an oasis of space for supporters' cars and heaved a satisfied sigh.

"We're here, Son," he smiled.

Mo trembled with excitement as they got out and stood in front of the high oval rise of the stadium. El Mokawloon's badge was emblazoned everywhere. In huge letters round the wall, a sign: *Welcome to the home of the Mountain Wolves*. Mo took a deep breath, steadying himself. Mountain Wolves was El Mokawloon's nickname. They had arrived and he wanted to belong more than anything.

"Your letter said to register at the Home Players' entrance," his dad said, knowing how best to calm his son down. "Which way?"

Mo swiveled the map that came with the joining instructions.

"That way," he said, trying to sound convincing.

His dad glanced down at the map and nodded. "Good. Let's go."

It took only a minute to find the Home Players' door. A tall, burly man in an old-fashioned blazer and tie stood on guard. Mo's dad showed him the joining letter from the club and the man smiled.

"Under 15s are on Pitch Three today, sir. They've already started." His gaze swept Mo up and down. "Go straight down. They'll fit your son with kit."

Out on Pitch Three, two lines of gawky youngsters ran and passed breathlessly. Handi Noor watched them closely. He was short and had a close-cropped beard and moustache. He didn't miss much. He spotted the approaching father and son out of the corner of his eye. He turned around. When he heard Mo's name, he smiled.

"Quick? Left foot like a thunderbolt?"

He looked Mo straight in the eye and shook his hand. Mo thought he would die of embarrassment.

"I watched you in Mahalla City once," Noor continued. "We'll see how you go here. Join the right-hand line. At the back."

"Yes, sir," Mo said, glancing at his dad and trotting off.

The drill was to run between two lines of cones, passing the ball back and forth to your partner while running, till you got to the first cone. Noor wanted it done at pace. As Mo joined, he heard the coach clapping loudly and shouting sternly.

"Mahmoud, pick up your feet!"

Mahmoud, a stocky lad who already had a thin moustache, put on a spurt as he ran from the top cone and joined Mo's line. He panted loudly with the effort, but his brow pursed inquisitively when he saw the new boy.

"Mohamed," Mo said, holding out his hand. "You can call me Mo."

"Mahmoud," the boy gasped. But he was too out of breath to go on. He put his hands down on his knees. The boy in front giggled, then shut up as he felt Noor's eye on him. He took Mo's outstretched hand.

"Youssouf," he said. "See what we are doing?"

Mo nodded. He started to jump and run on the spot, trying to get loose. His stomach was churning. When they got to the front of the line, Youssouf took the ball, booted it to his partner on the right, and ran off. It was Mo's turn now. He took a deep breath.

"Go," the assistant coach ordered. Mo set off. The ball skidded toward him. His heart pounded so much he thought it would burst.

The ball touched the outside of his left foot—and suddenly all Mo's tension vanished. As if in slow motion, he scooped the ball forward and side-footed in one easy movement, sending the ball precisely into the stride of his partner's run. When the ball came back to him, he did it again. And then again. It was like playing in a dream. He was at the first cone in no time rejoining the back of the line. Youssouf fist-bumped him.

"I can do it faster!" Mo said, matter-of-factly. Youssouf's eyes widened.

Mo's dad watched silently from the touchline as, for the next hour, Noor took the boys through more passing drills, and shooting and tackling. Mo was instantly one of the better ones, hanging on the coach's words. He performed every drill effortlessly, absorbed in the ball.

A tear moistened his eye.

It was a gamble, and his son would have to work hard. But it was what he wanted. The family would support Mo all the way. There was something special in him, and he was humble and sincere. He wondered what was in store for Mo. It all looked like a dream.

CHAPTER ELEVEN

"Do you want to be a pro?"

Mo slumped exhausted in the changing room.

There would be a bus from outside the stadium in three quarters of an hour, which would wind through the back streets of the Nasr City suburb to Cairo Central Station. Then it was three hours bumping along the straight road through the cotton fields to Tanta, a quarter hour wait for the bus to Basyoun, then the bike ride that was so familiar to him now. It would be midnight when he got home.

Then, at midday tomorrow, he would have to be back here at Osman Ahmad Osman stadium.

"See you, Mo!" Mahmoud came up and offered his open palm high then low. Mo roused himself and gave a cheery goodbye.

He had the furthest distance to travel home and was the last to leave. He yawned and started packing his bag.

The door opened. Handi Noor came through. For a moment he stood and watched while his latest recruit folded his boots, shorts, shirt, and socks into the bag. An open tin lay next to the bag, with the remains of some falafels, green salad, and pomegranate.

"Salah," he said, walking over and sitting down next to the teenager.

"Sir!" Mo said, sitting up straight.

Noor observed him keenly again, then asked without warning, "Let's talk before you go home. Do you have five minutes?"

"Yes, sir," Mo said as he sat straighter, his eyes riveted on Noor's face.

"I'm watching you closely as I watch all my players. You work very hard. You are talented. And you are a team player. But there are things you have to take care of if you want one day to become a pro. You have a lethal left foot. It's not enough. You should use your weak foot as often as your strong one. Practice with your right. I don't care if you muck up the drills."

"OK, sir," Mo said without hesitation.

"You must eat well and rest well. Do you understand?"

Mo nodded. He felt goose-bumps rising on the back of his neck.

"You must have no distractions. No late nights. No getting up late. No wandering on the streets. You must be wholly dedicated."

Mo nodded more slowly.

"Can you do this, Salah? It's not easy."

"Yes, sir."

Noor look at him straight into his eyes.

"The life of a professional is a life of sacrifice, Salah. There are talented ball players by the thousand, but only one in many has the guts to sacrifice everything. Prove to me that you're one of them, and I'll help you every way I can."

Mo swallowed. His guts twisted. Noor's words had banished all his tiredness. Still he had a four-hour journey home ahead of him.

Next day, he stayed on after official practice. It meant another midnight return home, but it didn't matter. He lined the cones up in front of the goal and began dribbling between them with his right foot only. When he got to the end, he twisted and put a shot in, just with his right.

The ball kept bobbling away from him. The shot missed.

He ran behind the net, picked the ball up with his right foot and controlled it slowly back to the beginning of the run. Then he tried again. Once more, the shot went wide.

Slower, he said to himself. For another two hours, he persevered. Bit by bit, the control got better. By the end, only half his shots were off target.

Handi Noor stood watching for the whole two hours, saying nothing. When Mo at last came off the pitch, he put his arm round the boy and gave him some notes. Mo listened intently, heart hammering again.

He wanted to tell his coach something that was on his mind. He played defense. The coach wanted him to stop the opponent and being one of the fastest players in the team, start a swift counterattack. But Mo wanted to be up front. He wanted to score and he thought that an attacking midfielder position would suit him much better. He hesitated and didn't say what was on his mind.

I'll find another opportunity, he thought.

The Mountain Wolves didn't practice on Friday, to allow everyone to attend prayers with their family. On Thursday night when he came home, Mo fell into bed as soon as dinner was over.

In the morning, when he came down early for breakfast, his dad greeted him with a sheet of paper and a wry grin.

"So, no more sleeping in for you, Son!" His eye twinkled. "Mr. Noor called me last night, and told me straight off you had a regime to follow if you want to make soccer your career!"

He pushed the paper over. And Mo glanced at it. His mom stood over him while he read it through.

"It's a lot," she said, "You are still so young."

"It's fine, Mom," Mo said. "It's what a pro should go through in order to succeed."

CHAPTER TWELVE

Striker!

Mo sweated under the floodlights at the Mountain Wolves stadium. As usual, he got up at six, cycled to school, studied for a few hours, and then left for the long snaking bus ride to Cairo. He felt the fatigue in his body. But he couldn't care less. He was doing what he wanted to do and he was happy.

He was fifteen now, playing for the Mountain Wolves Under-16s, with a new coach who reckoned his blistering pace and ball skills were ideally suited to closing down opposition attacks. It was well into the second half of the Wolves' fourth game of the 2007/08 Cairo Youth League season. Wolves were up two–one. At right back, Mo had run himself ragged keeping the ENPPI midfield under wraps. His crosses had led to the Mountain Wolves' goals. But he wasn't satisfied. He'd made a couple of runs out of defense, and not quite finished them off. It was frustrating.

Mountain Wolves' keeper rolled the ball to his feet. He was in a bit of space. He set off.

ENPPI's number ten came over off his wing to challenge. Mo took the ball past him with his right, easily. Handi Noor's training and all the practice last year were paying off.

Another player charged toward him next, but left a lot of room down the ENPPI right flank. Mo rifled the ball into it and forced himself to accelerate.

The ENPPI back four were no match even for a tired Mo Salah. The Wolves' defender reached the ball and one-touched it into the penalty area while they were still on the half-turn.

The keeper saw the danger and came off his line. Mo strained for the ball. He just needed to lift it. He felt the strain on his aching muscles. His stronger left foot got a touch but he wasn't close enough to the ball. His shot toed weakly into the falling keeper's chest.

Mo screamed at the sky in annoyance. The same thing for a *third* time!

He stopped dead, hands going to his knees, out of breath. The ENPPI keeper grinned as he booted the ball upfield.

At the final whistle, Mo was so down on himself he could hardly shake the opposition's hands. Twice more he'd managed to bring the ball out of defense and into a shooting position, only for his legs to fail at the crucial moment. Who cared that in that time, Mountain Wolves had scored another? Or that he'd made a goal-line block that stopped an ENPPI equalizer? He was frustrated and angry.

In the changing room, the head of youth teams, Said el-Shishini, congratulated everyone for their efforts. The victory left them riding high in the league. His teammates slapped each others' backs and sang as they stripped off their kit and cleaned up. Mo joined in as best as he could, but when everyone left, sank down to sit beneath his peg. His head fell between his knees, and tears flowed down his cheeks.

He felt a failure. How could he make it onto the El Mokawloon senior side, let alone beyond, if he fouled up so many golden opportunities?

"Mo!" el-Shishini's rumbling voice called him back to the present. Mo rubbed his eyes clear and made himself look up.

"My boy!" the older man said, noticing the streaks on Mo's face. He sat by him and put an arm round his shoulders.

"I'm so sorry, sir," Mo muttered. "I was terrible. I know it. I'm not good enough."

"Mo!" el-Shishini replied, shocked that his protege looked so disappointed. "You did great! You gave everything."

Mo managed to keep his voice steady. "Effort isn't enough if I mess up."

"Mo, you were my man of the match," el-Shishini insisted. "Your performance is the reason we won. If you'd scored even one of those goals, it would only have been the icing on the cake."

Mo frowned. He couldn't understand the praise.

"No-one else could have made those opportunities, my boy," el-Shishini went on, reaching into his pocket and pulling out his wallet. He fished out a twenty Egyptian pound note and offered them. "Your man of the match prize."

Mo took the money in wonder.

"I owe you an apology," el-Shishini continued. "It's my fault you couldn't finish those chances. You had too much work to do moving the ball up. I've obviously been playing you out of position. You should be further up. You are a natural attacking midfielder. I think you'll make a great striker, but I want you under the striker because you are so fast."

Mo looked struck. He knew this all along. But it was so much better that his coach realized it himself.

"Even though I missed all those chances?" he said with a lighter mood.

His coach nodded. "After tonight, you'll play number nine. And my prediction is you'll score goals. Lots of goals. It wouldn't surprise me if you top this year's league."

Mo closed his eyes, his heart beating fast. "I'll do my best, sir," he said. "I won't let you down."

CHAPTER THIRTEEN

A Real Pro

His coach was right. When the season finished in May 2008, Mo was top goal-scorer in both the Cairo Youth League and the All Egypt Youth League. After the last training session, el-Shishini called him into his office.

"When do you turn sixteen, Salah?" he asked.

"Couple of weeks," Mo replied.

"Good," el-Shishini rumbled. "I won't have to wait long for your signature."

He handed him an envelope. "It's a professional contract. We want you on our senior squad. Talk it over with your family."

Mo felt the envelope in his hand and overflowed with gratitude.

"It's a big decision," el-Shishini went on. "You'd get lodgings here at the academy. No more back and forth. But it means leaving home."

Mo turned the envelope over in his fingers. *Leave Nagrig? Leave his family?*

"Here's my home number," el-Shishini rumbled on, "your father can call me any time."

Mo waited for the bus journey that night to come to an end as soon as possible. He wanted to show the contract to his parents and get their approval. He played in his head the conversation. *They must say yes,* he thought. He yearned to hear them say it and he tried to picture their reaction.

But when he got home around midnight, no one was up, and he had to wait before breaking the news. When he woke up, he ran to his parents with the envelope.

He waved it in front of them. "A contract," he said. "They want to sign me."

They hugged him. His mom held him tightly while she heard her husband read the contract out loud, then set him away from her, hands on his arms.

"It's a just reward for working so hard," she said. "We'll be here, whenever you need us. Your coach is a good man, and he'll look after you."

"Is it what you want, Son?" his dad asked with tears in his eyes, although he knew the answer.

Mo nodded.

A month later, he sat on the familiar bus, a suitcase in front of him. This time he knew that he wouldn't be coming back that night. His heart ached. He had to make a sacrifice to do what he loved most. And he was determined to make the most out of it.

In August, Mo Salah transitioned to the El Mokawloon Under-20 team. He liked watching and working with the more experienced players. By May the following year, as the season drew to a close, he felt he'd made modest progress.

He came off Pitch Three, where the Wolves had been playing Al-Ahly. The game was a draw and it was his assist that led to Mountain Wolves Under-20's only goal. He wasn't happy and felt he could have done better.

He spurted water from the bottle down his throat and let some play over his face. He made his way quietly to the changing room and freshened up.

Yassir el-Batouni, a larger than life player, came up to him with an offer.

"Mo, do you want to come out tonight? We're going to see Hamada Hilal. He's singing in the open on Tahrir Square."

Mo was tempted. He loved music, and Hilal's music made you want to dance.

"When does he play?"

"Oh, you know—eleven, twelve. We might take in a dance club first."

Mo frowned. He liked to keep Handi Noor's regime going, in spite of all the distractions of culture here in the big city. If Hilal didn't start till midnight, it would be close to dawn by the time they all got back.

He shook his head. "Too late for me. I'll be too tired."

"Come on, Mo. You're only young once. Let's have some fun!"

Yassir was a good player, but not ambitious. Mo smiled, wide and engaging, and shook his head again.

"See you in the morning, Yassir. Have fun."

He walked down to the stadium café for dinner. They did a good fried chicken, soup, and green salad there, which reminded him of home. Then he went to his room, number 510. It looked out on the stadium itself. Often, he would do nothing except look out at the pitch, dreaming.

Tonight, he planned to do an hour or two of FIFA 2008 on his PlayStation, He liked to play Steven Gerrard, striking impossible long-range goals that weren't like his own at all. Then he would call home.

Before he could settle, his phone rang.

"Mo?" It was Said el-Shishini. "Where are you?"

"In my room, sir."

"Good. Sit down, my boy. Good news. You're needed for the First Team briefing at seven a.m. Musa, our Nigerian midfielder, pulled a thigh muscle in training. Alaa Nabil wants you to replace him on the bench."

Mo could hardly believe his ears. Nabil was El Mokawloon's manager.

"Get a good night's sleep, my boy. They'll put you on in the second half."

Sleep was the last thing on Mo's mind that night. He put on a Hilal tune. "Good enough."

Back home in Nagrig, after Mo's call, his dad announced the big news and everyone cheered.

"Mo Salah, seventeen, makes his Egyptian Premier League debut!"

CHAPTER FOURTEEN

An Unforgettable Moment!

"Watch this one, Bob!" Ibrahim Mahleb shouted above the noise of the expectant home crowd. "He's never scored, but it's just a matter of time."

It was December 25, 2010, a normal warm midwinter day in Egypt. Mahleb, the Mountain Wolves' President, pointed from his Director's box at a fresh-faced youngster running out onto the pitch with the rest of the team. Bob Bradley, the American manager of Egypt's national soccer team, smiled cautiously back. He wanted to form his own opinion about this eighteen-year-old, Mohamed Salah.

"Bob," Mahleb continued, as Mountain Wolves lined up alongside El-Ahly, the league leaders. "I want to find a hero. A son of Egypt taking the whole world by storm. Exciting as a soccer player. Humble as a man. Someone to represent us, and make us proud to be Egyptian. Unite us. Rich or poor. Zamaleki or El-Ahlili. The country needs it." He paused. "I really believe it could be that young man."

"That's admirable, sir," Bradley said, then changed the subject. "And I sure could do with a playmaker who scores goals."

The match kicked off.

It was a typical Egyptian Premier League game. Fast, footloose, and imaginative, but lacking in structure. At the end of a scoreless first half, neither team had imposed themselves. As the players strode off, the Mountain Wolves' striker nudged Mo.

"Mr. Bradley's watching us. Doesn't it make you nervous?"

Mo gave the shy smile that was already becoming his trademark.

"I'd like to make our fans happy," he said.

Midway through the second half, El-Ahly went one up from a free-kick. Five minutes later, after a streaking run which won his team a corner, Mo Salah found himself with the ball on the edge of the crowded El-Ahly box, back to the goal. There was no-one to lay it off to. He spun in a heartbeat, saw a gap through the forest of legs, and threaded the ball sweetly through it.

"Goal!!" The entire stadium erupted like a volcano.

"Neat strike!" Bradley exclaimed. Mahleb celebrated with a roar, dancing in circles as if he was just an ordinary fan.

It was Mo Salah's introduction to the Egyptian Premier League. He just stood there smiling while the entire team piled on him.

A star was born.

A few days later, Mo pulled his tracksuit on after training when his mobile rang. After he finished, he sat down speechless, looked heavenward, his face wreathed in a grateful smile.

"What happened?" a fellow player said.

"It was Mr. Bradley," he savored the words. "They want me for the National Under-20's Squad." It was a joy like nothing he'd ever experienced.

Immediately the whole team surrounded him, hammering his back. "Yalla, Salah!" someone shouted. "Go for it!"

"About time," Alaa Nabil said, laying two hands on Mo's shoulders. "You deserve it."

Mo called Nagrig straight away, and when he hung up, he said breathlessly and soberly, "God gives with one hand and corrects us with another, sir. My family's home in Nagrig was burgled last night. I should go to them."

Nabil nodded. "Yes, my boy. Take some time off. Go home and help your family."

As Mo took the familiar bus journey to his hometown, he couldn't help comparing his own good fortune to the thief, who the police had caught. He knew who it was. In Nagrig, everyone knew everyone. It was a boy of sixteen, leaving secondary education with no qualifications and no chances of a job. He came from a large family who'd lost their father. They lived in a two-room flat, six children, mother and grandmother. Mo felt bad for him.

The sun was setting when he arrived at Nagrig. Before going to his parents', Mo visited Maggi. He wanted to talk about the burglary. But Maggi had other plans.

"I heard you're going to play for Egypt!" she said happily, leading him upstairs to the balcony of her family's house.

"Oh that," Mo replied. "Maybe. If I keep playing well enough."

Maggi laughed. "Stop, Mo! Of course you're gonna play great!"

Mo smiled. "Thanks, but did you hear about the burglary?"

She nodded gravely. "Everyone knows. Your father says the boy deserves jail."

Mo pursed his lips. "Maggi, it's hard for me to say this, but I don't think Dad's right. The boy was just trying to help his family and couldn't think of anything else to do. He was desperate. What if … what if I were to talk to him … give him some money—to help him? I have enough. It might save him. What do you think?"

Maggi looked at Mo and a lump came into her throat. "I think you are going to make me cry, Mo. That's so brave and beautiful. God will surely bless you."

He blushed. "Please. Be serious."

"I am," she said and hugged him and whispered: "Do it."

He stood up. "I haven't talked with Dad yet. Will you come with me?"

She nodded. "Of course."

CHAPTER FIFTEEN

South Africa Here We Come!

It was the first time Mo had ever thought about someone else and he never forgot it. When the story got around Nagrig, it made him even more of a hero than being picked for Egypt's side.

It was on his mind as the Boeing 737 rose out of Cairo International Airport later in the year, carrying him and twenty-two other excited teenagers to South Africa, for the African Youth Cup. *In my country,* he thought, *soccer gives people joy, still it's not enough. They need so much more.*

He had his PlayStation, but for the whole eight-hour flight he was thinking about his life. He knew that he wanted to make a difference. But how?

It was his first time in the air and his first time outside Egypt. The enormous scale of his home continent, Africa, beat into him. Below, arid highlands gave way slowly to wide prairies then vast, snow-capped mountains surrounded by an ocean of jungle. They spent an hour flying down a huge band of lakes. After that was more jungle, more prairie, another desert, bare and desolate, then, at last, the sunbaked coast of their destination.

The Egyptian youngsters went deep into the tournament. First Lesotho, then South Africa fell to the Young Pharaohs. They were through to the semi-finals.

On the afternoon of April 28, 2011, Mo Salah stood in the middle of a huddle in the changing rooms of Johannesburg's Dobsonville stadium. In five minutes, they would face Cameroon in the semi-finals.

"We can do this. We can be heroes for our country," he said, intensely. "Work together. Press hard. Pass quickly. Yalla, el-Masr! Come on, Egypt!"

They ran out, believing.

Sadly, on the field of play, the other team had strong beliefs as well and things didn't go Egypt's way. After a scoreless game, they lost 4–2 on penalties. In the dejected atmosphere beneath the stands afterward, Mo spoke out again. "We can still win a medal," he said to his teammates. "Let's not give up."

The bronze disks hung around his neck by the FIFA President the next week was Mo's first ever honor. He felt a moment of satisfaction as the team paraded their prize in front of the few hundred traveling fans in a corner of the stadium. But on the flight home, he put all thoughts of the tournament behind him and continued to think about his destiny. About his future. After wearing his country's uniform in his biggest soccer tournament ever, he knew he wanted to do it in the World Cup. He was thinking about his future again and again. God gifted him with this talent. He needed to give back to his people. When the plane prepared to land, he thought, *I want to be the greatest soccer player in Egypt's history. This is my destiny.*

When he came out of customs at Cairo Airport, he was surprised to find a dozen photographers and several TV crews covering the Under-20 team's return. A small crowd of supporters chanted their success. As Mo made his way past them, a boy ran up to him, closely followed by his father.

"Can you sign your name, sir?" the boy asked, shyly extending a notepad and a pen.

For a second, Mo froze. No-one had ever asked for his autograph.

"You're my favorite player!" the boy told him. "I want to score like you when I grow up!"

Mo signed and said to the boy, "Thank you."

In the second half of the year, his name started to resonate around the country. He played his first matches in the international team, scoring the last goal in Egypt's three-nil win over Niger. At Mountain Wolves, he was scoring nearly a goal every two games. As he grew in stature, Ibrahim Mahleb watched over him with pride and hope. That's when Zamalek called the Mountain Wolves President and talked to him about selling Mo to them.

CHAPTER SIXTEEN

Leaving

"No! A thousand times, no!"

The Mountain Wolves President slammed the phone down and moodily picked up the remote control in front of him. That was the third time Zamalek Soccer Club had tried to entice him into selling Mo Salah.

He would not do it. Mo deserved better than the Egyptian league. He needed stronger competition that would push him to become so much better. He'd explained that to Mo, the first time Zamalek came calling, at the end of the 2011 season.

He watched the news on TV. Forty-seven fans had died during riots at a soccer match in the town of Port Said. He was sad and disgusted and let out a sigh of despair. Then he caught sight of the words scrolling across the bottom of the screen. *All* remaining matches of the Egyptian Premier League canceled for the season. He had known the Egyptian FA's decision in advance. Now it was out in the open.

He turned off the TV and got up from his desk.

Zamalek would no doubt be badgering his best player with their latest offer, despite his resistance. But in the uncertainty following the cancelation of the whole season, who knew what the young Mo Salah would think. He was, after all, humble. A good boy. He'd want to do what was best for his family.

Mahleb strode down from the office levels to the youth players lodgings where Mo still lived. He stopped by Room 510. He knocked, then went in without waiting for a reply. Mo was sitting on his bed, head in hands. His mobile lay on the bed.

"I know what you're thinking," Mahleb said without preamble. "What use is a contract when I can't actually play any soccer."

He sat next to Mo and put a comforting arm round the young man's shoulders. Mo was shaking his head, his face a mask of frustration.

"You trust me, Mohamed Salah?" Mahleb said, giving Mo's shoulders a shake. Mo looked up.

"Of course."

"You believe me when I tell you that you'll go on from here. I know Zamalek have been calling."

Mo shook his head urgently.

"Sir, I don't listen to them. It's not that. It's the Olympics. We need match-fitness. How will we get it now? How can we make Egypt proud after that terrible day?"

In only four months, the 2012 London Olympics soccer tournament would begin. Egypt's Under-23 side were fancied to do well.

Mahleb grunted. "You're right. You do need competitive matches." He thought for a moment while Mo hung his head, dejected. Then he stood up. "Mo, keep your training as intense as if we were still playing. I'll get you matches."

Mahleb was as good as his word. The Under-23 training camp started early and after three weeks, their manager Hany Ramzy, a former international, stood in front of the squad and announced a series of warm-up games, starting with a trip to Switzerland, to play F.C. Basel.

When the team arrived at Basel and settled in their hotel, Mo noticed the differences from home; the prosperity and orderliness and the cold. He found himself shivering as he waited on the bench in the first half of the match.

Basel had some good players, internationals, and the German virtues of teamwork and organization. At the half-time break, the Young Pharaohs hadn't managed to break their defense. Ramzy told Mo he was going on. Mo made an impact almost as soon as he stepped on the pitch. He scored two goals by the end of the game, as the Egyptian youngsters ran out victors.

Unknown to him, Ibrahim Mahleb was not only pulling strings to get the Egyptian team some match play. As the players gathered for their post-match debrief, he made his way into the Egyptian changing room and came up to Mo.

"Mo. What a game you played out there. Impressive. Can I have a word with you?"

Confused, Mo rose. Hany Ramzy, the U-23 manager nodded to him encouragingly as he followed Mahleb through the door. What could it be about?

Outside, he recognized Heiko Vogel, Basel's manager. He'd seen the man pacing the touchline during the game. Vogel stepped forward, extending his hand.

"Mr. Salah, I'm very pleased to meet you at last," he said slowly, in English. "Mr. Mahleb talked to us about you over a year ago. We've followed you ever since. Will you stay here for a week, for a trial? If it goes well, we'd like to sign you."

Mo looked at the man and he thought about the words he just heard.

They want me. Here in Basel.

"Thank you, sir," he said. "It's a great opportunity. I'll discuss it with my parents."

When he was back at the hotel, he made the phone call home.

"When are you coming home?" his mom asked.

"I'm not. I'm staying here. Only for a week..."

He told them about the Basel proposal. Thousands of miles away he could hear their excitement. He couldn't blame them. He was excited too. They were longing to have him back home. When he hung up, he felt joy and sadness. Outside his room, the night was cold and misty. He wasn't sure he was ready to leave his family and Egypt behind. But deep in his heart he knew it was his calling. Another milestone on his road to greatness.

A month later, he sat in a Cairo café with Ibrahim Mahleb opposite. Basel had offered a four-year contract.

"Am I ready?" he asked.

"You're humble, Mo," Mahleb said. "And modest. That's good. But don't let it hold you back. Don't hesitate. Accept the offer."

"I've dreamed of playing in Europe since I was little," Mo said. "But I never imagined ... I don't speak any German! I won't know a single soul there."

Mahleb smiled. "You will find it hard, Mo, but God willing you will prevail. They're good people and it's a great club. They'll look after you. You'll learn so much. You will become a man." He leaned across the table and touched Mo's arm. "And the money is huge."

Mo closed his eyes. He seemed to hear his dad's voice, asking him to look into his heart that day he had to leave Nagrig for good. His heart gave him the same reply as then. He gave Mahleb a determined look.

"I'll sign. And God willing I'll prevail."

"You shall," Mahleb beamed with pride. "You'll do well, for yourself and for all Egyptians."

By the end of April, Mo was on the plane to Switzerland.

CHAPTER SEVENTEEN

Basel

"Ready Mo?"

Fabian Frei's English was as heavily accented as Mo's, but it was their only common language. Frei played alongside Mo in F.C. Basel's midfield. He was one of Basel's own, coming up through their youth system. Like Mo, he had just come back from the Olympics. Above them, at the end of the tunnel, St. Jakob Park stadium heaved with supporters waving red and blue scarves.

Mo nodded, eyes focused, bouncing on his toes. It was the middle of August, his second start for his new team, a home game versus Lausanne in the Super League, Switzerland's top division.

The London Olympics was already just a memory. Egypt did creditably: a victory, a draw and a defeat in the group stage; a losing quarter-final against Japan in front of 70,000 spectators at Old Trafford. Mo had done most of the scoring in so far and wanted more.

Mo scampered onto the pitch into a light rain and began his routine. It was three months since he arrived in Basel. He wasn't yet fully used to their system but he was learning fast. Thankfully, he scored in the first time he'd turned out, a pre-season friendly against Steaua Bucureșt.

The game started and he felt immediately at home. In the second half, Mo made a darting run into the box from the right wing and met Fabian Frei's cross with his left. It flew into the net. His first Super League goal!

Mo ran exultantly back up the pitch after being surrounded by his team. In his joy, he instinctively fell to his knees and put his forehead to the ground, thanking God. As they came off the pitch, Frei shook his hand and made a point of congratulating him on his whole play. Vogel threw his arms round Mo's shoulders.

"Good game!" he said. "Good looking round!" He pointed to his eyes. "Good space!" He made a sweeping gesture round his body.

That was how they were at Basel. Always making a huge effort to include him and explain, despite the language barrier. Mo appreciated it. He smiled brightly back.

"Thank you, sir! I keep learning!"

After the match, Mo went for a walk, needing something to fill the sixteen hours before training began the next day. It got him out of his hotel room and got him used to the city. Everything was so different than home. All those immaculately painted buildings! All those tidy shops! He got lost in the pine forest on the edge of town, listening to the rain drip off the branches. It was so quiet. When he came out, he felt a little less lonely.

That day, as he strolled back to the hotel, a group of men in red and blue Basel scarves came striding down the street toward him. They were big, burly men, with cropped hair and stubble, in jeans and T-shirts. Suddenly, one stopped and stared in Mo's direction. He shouted something.

Mo felt anxious. The man shouted again. "Mohamed Salah!"

Mo nodded, still nervous.

The man's face broke into a huge smile. He rolled up to Mo, talking fast, holding out his hand. Mo felt his fingers crushed and smiled, but his face showed he didn't understand the words. The man frowned.

"Goal!" he said, in English, punching the air and pointing at Mo. "Thank you!"

Then he rejoined his companions, turning back several times to wave with his thumbs up.

It was a fan! Mo laughed to himself and walked back to his hotel with a new feeling of determination to overcome his loneliness.

"You'll have to get used to the fans," Maggi laughed, when he told her the story over the phone.

As the year went on, she was proved right. Mo's picture appeared often on the news. Lots of people recognized him in the streets. When he took the cable ferry, men wanted to shake his hand and talk about the games. He had many conversations in halting English, or even simpler German.

It wasn't just in Basel.

He'd scored ten goals as Basel cruised to a Swiss Super League title, came runners up in the Swiss Cup, and made the semi-finals of the Europa League. He was the African Soccer Confederation's most promising talent of 2012. UEFA gave him a Golden Boot award.

After a year away, Mo came home to Nagrig in June 2013. When his dad took him and Nasr to Uncle's café, the place erupted.

"That goal against Chelsea!" Abadah laughed, as they embraced. "The walls shook so much I thought the TV would fall down!"

Abadah was helping Uncle now.

Mo just shook his head. All these smiling faces. He was glad to make them happy.

Later, he strolled out to the soccer court, with Maggi. Some boys were out kicking a ball about. One spotted Mo and his eyes went like saucers.

"Mohamed Salah!" he bellowed. Mo went red. The boy's face lit up and he gestured invitingly to the ball at his feet. Mo looked at Maggi. He couldn't resist. Just like in his childhood, he jumped through the gap in the wall and sprinted onto the pitch. For half-an-hour, he played. Passing the ball back and forth, making it talk. He picked the boys out one by one, directing them where to go, laughing at his own mistakes. Maggi watched smiling.

As they walked back home, he asked her to marry him.

"I thought you'd never ask!" she said.

CHAPTER EIGHTEEN

London Calls

Barry Hunter, Anfield's head scout, hunched against the fall chill. He was high up in the stands at Chelsea to watch a young Egyptian midfielder. The lad played for F.C. Basel, drawn in Chelsea's group in the Champions League. Mo Salah was the player's name. Skillful. Quick. Worked hard. Hat-trick versus Zimbabwe in a World Cup qualifier. Worth checking.

The London Club were one-nil up going into the last quarter, seemingly cruising.

Mo controlled a long ball close to the penalty area and skipped past the England captain, John Terry. He looked up and side-footed calmly past a diving Petr Cech in the Chelsea goal.

It was decisive. Ten minutes later, Mo worked hard down the right flank and got the ball into the box. Streller made it two for the Swiss team.

Back at Anfield, Hunter insisted they monitor Mo Salah more closely.

"Look at these plays against Maccabi Tel Aviv," he said, flicking through videos of Basel's home and away Champions League qualifiers.

"Always creating problems, making chances. See that strike, takes the pass from Hassler on his own. one, two touches, and bang. With the side of the foot too. We could do with that."

Dave Fallows, Liverpool's head of recruitment glanced at the sporting director Michael Edwards. "Keep your eye on him then."

But it was not Liverpool who took Mo away from Basel.

Three minutes from the end of Basel's home leg against Chelsea, Mo dinked an onrushing Cech to beat the Czech keeper a second time. It was the only goal of the match. Added to the strikes against his team the year before, it was too much for the Chelsea manager, Jose Mourinho, to stomach. He went to straight to Roman Abramovich, Chelsea's owner.

"Mohamed Salah is fast, creative, enthusiastic," Mourinho explained. "Besides, he keeps scoring goals against us! I think we need him."

"So, buy him," Abramovich purred.

Mo knew nothing about the English Premier League Club's interest as he left for Egypt when the Swiss Super League's winter break began. His mind was full of only one thing—marrying Maggi.

"It looks like Dad invited the whole of Nagrig," he joked into Maggi's ears, while he twirled her round the dance floor.

"And your favorite singers," she replied. In the background, Hamada Hilal and Abdel Basset Hamouda duetted. Around them, the men of the family gathered in a circle, clapping and twirling in time to the booming drums.

The celebration went on all night.

When Mo went back to Basel, Mourinho's people were waiting. Mo could hardly believe the money they were willing to offer, but that wasn't the dealmaker for him. The English Premier League was considered the best in the world. Moving there would mean playing alongside and against some of the greatest players in the world. He would work with Mourinho and his coaching team. His game would have to get better. It would make him a bigger asset for his country. He decided to sign with the Blues.

Mo joined Chelsea on January 26, 2014. The same month, Maggi announced that she was pregnant. Mo was still on a high three months later when he stepped out onto the pitch at Anfield, in Chelsea's away fixture against Liverpool. In the last four weeks, he'd scored his first two goals for Chelsea and picked up two Man of the Match awards. Facing him was Steven Gerrard, the man who only four years ago he picked out to be on his FIFA PlayStation. The atmosphere was unbelievable. The sound of the Kop as they sang "You'll Never Walk Alone" before kick-off brought tears to his eyes.

He played like a man possessed; and although he didn't score, Chelsea did, twice, on the break, against almost constant Liverpool pressure. The victory brought Chelsea tantalizingly close to the top of the table.

For Mo, everything was a dream come true. He was playing well and learning.

In a month, he would be going home to put his new Premier League wages to work building a pitch for the Nagrig youngsters.

And Maggi was going to have their first baby.

CHAPTER NINETEEN

Crash

Mo ran on the spot, slapping his arms round his shoulders. Chelsea were in the tunnel of Shrewsbury Town F.C.'s New Meadow ground, about to run out for their English League Cup second round tie. It wasn't Chelsea's most important game, but it mattered more to Mo than any other since coming to London.

The year which had started so well was now a struggle. After the Anfield game, Chelsea's Premier League 2013/14 title chase went west. They ended the season without a trophy. An unhappy Mourinho let the dressing room know just how disappointed he was. Mo had never heard such contempt in a boss's voice. It was embarrassing.

In July, when he went back home for Ramadan, he got a letter from the Egyptian Ministry of Education. It said his student registration was canceled, and he had to report to the Army for three years of military service. Every young man in Egypt had to unless they had an exemption.

Mo was in despair. Soccer was his way to benefit Egypt on the world stage that Chelsea would give him. It looked like everything would be taken away. He didn't understand.

"Surely I can serve my country better as a soccer player?" he told his dad in bewilderment.

They were in Abadah's café, looking at the school soccer pitch plans.

"Maybe your Mountain Wolves boss can help," his dad mused. "Ibrahim Mahleb is Prime Minister now."

It took nearly two months of negotiations, which he could do nothing to influence, before the Ministry of Education changed its mind.

Now, two months into the new season, Chelsea were running away with the League but not because of Mo. He'd played only eighteen minutes of the first team. It wasn't unexpected. Mo's rivals for the attacking midfield spot, Eden Hazard and Diego Costa were both Golden Boot nominees. But it was hard for Mo to warm the bench. He was desperate for people to see his game. Sitting on the bench was depressing. He really wanted to play but he didn't get the minutes.

Shrewsbury Town were two divisions below Chelsea, an out of the way club in the bleak and damp countryside. They had no big names. The stands were rusty and leaking. Only about a thousand Chelsea fans had made the three-hour journey from London for the League Cup fourth-round game. It was like El Mokawloon going to play Ittihad Basyoun. Mo ran out in front of a small but vociferous and hostile crowd.

Mourinho's ice-cold words in the dressing room echoed in his ears. "I expect players who have not played much to show up for the game."

He means me, Mo thought. He tried to keep his enthusiasm to do well in check.

Right from the kick off, everything felt wrong. The Shrewsbury team had nothing to lose. They contested every ball as fiercely as if their lives depended on it and put together some slick, simple moves of their own. What should have been a cakewalk turned into a mud wrestle.

Just before half-time, it was still scoreless. Mo found himself in space on the right wing. Instinctively, he surged downfield and cut inside, leaving his marker for dead. Looking up, he saw the keeper ill-positioned.

Now he could show his game.

He snapped off a shot with his left.

To his horror, as he swung, his boot scuffed the turf. The ball ballooned off the outside of his foot, high and wide and went out for a throw-in.

Mo stared in disbelief.

The Shrewsbury Town fans erupted in jeers, shouting "Eeyore" at him as if he was a donkey.

At half-time, Mourinho brought Didier Drogba on. Three minutes into the second half, Mo found a line down the right flank and pinged a through ball to him. The Cameroon striker made no mistake.

In the dressing room afterward, Mourinho didn't look at Mo.

For the next four months, Mo worked harder on the training field than he had ever done. His fellow midfielders in the squad, Eden Hazard, Cesc Fabregas, Oscar, and Willian appreciated the effort, but it was obvious Mourinho didn't trust him. Even the goals Mo scored for Egypt in the Africa Cup of Nations qualifiers made no impression.

New Year came, and Mo had played only one more game for Chelsea.

At the end of January 2015, Steve Holland, Mourinho's English Assistant Manager, sat down with him.

"No beating round the bush," Holland said, "you're having a tough time."

Mo looked at Holland warily.

"Warming the bench all the time, it's not a good feeling," Holland said.

I'm not in the match-day squad at all! Mo thought.

"Mr. Mourinho wants you to know that all your efforts for the team are much appreciated," Holland went on.

Mo mustered up a muttered thanks. He knew he should feel grateful, but what he wanted was games.

"We want you to get more playing time. We really do," Holland continued. "So, how would you feel about a move? To Italy? A loan, not a transfer. You'd still be on our books."

Mo blinked. Moving him? It was like a knife in his guts. Worse than being dropped. It meant they didn't want him.

"We want to bring a striker in," Holland carried on. "A finisher. We've found someone at Fiorentina—and *they* want someone to make chances. That's you. They're prepared to do a swap. How'd you feel about that?"

Mo thought it was a rejection, no doubt about it. It felt like starting all over again. It made him feel angry. But Fiorentina were a Serie A club. If it meant getting regular play again … he should swallow his anger, be humble, not refuse the chance.

"How long?" he said, quietly.

"A couple of seasons and you'll be back in London during the summer."

Mo nodded at Holland with hard, determined eyes. He would make this work. "OK," he said, his face ashen.

"Good man," Holland smiled. "Now, just remember one thing. Italian defenders will eat you for breakfast unless you're strong." He looked at Mo's still slim physique. "If I were you, I'd start stuffing yourself with pasta, and hitting the weights."

CHAPTER TWENTY

SIM SALAH BIS!

The café was his regular stop jogging down the cobbled alleyways from his flat toward the Fiorentina training ground in the beautiful city of Florence. Mo put down the *Gazetta del Sport,* laughing to himself. *Sim Salah bis!* the headline said. It meant *Abracadabra* and fitted his own name in at the same time.

"What a crazy goal!" the barista enthused, pushing Mo's espresso over the counter.

The night before, Mo's temporary team, nicknamed the Viola, played Juventus in the semi-final of the Coppa Italia. The goal had been fun, like being back on the streets again. It started with Juve's Simone Pepe swinging a corner into Fiorentina's box. The Violas got to it first, hoofing the ball high and mighty downfield.

Mo was lurking. With the ball at his feet, he realized there was no-one between him and the Juventus goal, sixty meters away. He exploded.

His run arced from midway in Fiorentina's half, cross field, right to left, his pace deceptively easy and uncatchable. The one Juve defender not pressing the attack got burned almost before he could move. As Mo approached the penalty area, he slowed only a fraction.

The legendary Gianluigi Buffon, in goal for Juve, rushed off his line, spreading his arms and legs like an eagle about to pounce.

Mo took no notice.

Calmly, leaving Buffon no hope, he curled the ball off his left foot into the far bottom corner of the net.

The end-to-end strike had the stadium rocking.

"I like to make people happy!" Mo said to the barista, as he downed the espresso and waved goodbye.

Even better was what Fiorentina's manager, Vincenzo Montella, told him. "What a decisive strike! Chelsea never told us you had ice water in your veins!"

Mo reflected that he'd tried too hard at Chelsea. All he needed was to relax, and concentrate on what was in front of him. It made him a better player.

That summer, after nine goals in twenty-six games, he checked back in at Stamford Bridge. Mourinho and Mo sat in the spacious players' lounge overlooking the stadium. A couple of days short of his twenty-third birthday, Mo realized that Mourinho no longer overawed him. He smiled his widest, freshest smile. The Chelsea manager returned it with a characteristically shrewd, calculating look.

"You don't want a transfer to Fiorentina? It's a good offer."

Mo didn't reply instantly. He knew that Fiorentina were keen to make his move there permanent. But in his mind, he replayed the conversation he'd had on the phone a couple of weeks previously, with the Roma manager, Luciano Spaletti. The man's warmth immediately made him feel at home. What he said about Mo's game intrigued Mo even more. He talked about positioning, awareness, and strength. It was everything Mo knew he needed to work on.

"I want to be pushed harder," he told Mourinho.

His mind looked ahead, to the coming two years of internationals for Egypt: Africa Cup of Nations followed by the World Cup, qualifiers, and tournaments. Young as he was, they would look to him for leadership.

"You don't like Mr. Montella?" Mourinho said, eyeing him shrewdly. "Someone else is better?"

Mo knew Mourinho well enough now that he simply waited for the manager's next move. Mourinho sat back in his chair, then laughed.

"You've grown up, Mo. Good. So, you know Roma are offering us more than Fiorentina, but only a loan. I think their style suits *you* more. Is that right?"

"I have a responsibility, sir," Mo said. "For my country as well as to myself. There's so much I have to improve. Mr. Spaletti, I think, can help me get where I need to be. Besides … Totti was my childhood hero."

Mourinho chuckled harshly, then his face turned decisive. "Done. But your loan period at Roma ends at the end of next season."

"Thank you, sir." Mo stood up, offering his hand. Mourinho simply nodded.

CHAPTER TWENTY-ONE

More Famous Than Totti!

Mo sat with his cousin Abadah in the café back in Nagrig. He was there for Ramadan, after a tour of Egypt with the whole Roma team at the end of his first season in Italy. He felt contented. The time at Roma was everything he'd hoped for. Top scorer. Player of the Year. The loan turned into a permanent contract. Best of all, Egypt were going to the Africa Cup of Nations, largely because of his goals, including away games in Tanzania after the Serie A season finished.

Outside, youngsters were running to and fro on the all-weather pitch.

"Tell me everything, Mr. Pepsi!" Ab said. "Tell me about Totti."

Mo laughed. They were watching the new Pepsi advert, which Mo starred in, alongside Ab and the café: a scene of everyone cheering as Mo scored for Roma. Mo loved the advert, with its message to Asian and African youngsters. "Believe."

"Francesco?" Mo smiled. "He's everything we imagined, Ab. Always thinking about where he can impose himself as a player. He shows me a lot. He has his own charity too."

The screen flickered. Now it played footage of Mo in play. The Palermo game. Mo grinned. He remembered that one. He was through into the penalty area, at maximum speed, but still had more than one defender as well as the keeper to beat.

That was when all his extra work with Spaletti after the rest of the team's training paid off. It was about reading the spaces even if it meant going somewhere impossible.

None of the Roma players were with him, because his break had been so incisive. Palermo's back line were closing him down. But there was space all the way over on the opposite corner of the area, at the by-line.

So that was where he directed the ball, searing past the keeper on a crazy angle, collecting it just before it went out, midway between the six-yard box and the edge of the area, then turning. It gave him an open shot at goal, although from that angle all he could see was the post.

He hit the ball softly, exquisitely. It curled into the middle of the net.

Abadah shook his head. "That is why your picture is painted everywhere! Genius!"

"In'sh'allah," Mo said. "It's all God's grace."

"You are more famous than Totti now!" Abadah went on.

Mo shook his head. It was unbelievable, although probably true. During the tour, the Egyptian youngsters mobbed him, not the legendary Italian. He didn't feel big-headed about it. He knew the kids came up to him because he gave them hope. The saw themselves in him. They were the same as he was at nine or ten. Kicking a ball barefoot, watching games on TV. He showed them what an ordinary Egyptian could accomplish, with focus, hard work, and humility.

"I will have to put a painting of you on the wall," Ab joked. "Like the place I went to in Cairo. Then people will come here for selfies and my café will be as famous as you. Maybe I will rename it, 'Mo Salah's Coffee Paradise'".

"Be serious!" Mo laughed.

"I am!" Ab insisted. "But maybe 'Mo Salah's Happiness Café' is better. What do you think? It's what they are calling you, you know. Mr. Happiness-Maker."

He knew that. The Mayor told him. It started after Maggi and Mo funded a local school for the town girls who in the past were traveling out of Nagrig just to get a basic education.

"Please. Stop talking about it, Ab!" Mo's face was red with embarrassment. "I'm glad to give something back—but if you praise me too much, I will get too big for my britches."

"You?" Ab laughed. "You're much too modest."

"You don't understand," Mo said. "This is home. I want to feel comfortable here. Not on display."

Ab looked at him keenly. "My friend, it *is* your home. And we will joke with you any time and make you feel like one of us still. But you gotta realize we're going to show you off too!"

CHAPTER TWENTY-TWO
Liverpool!

"I like this player," Jurgen Klopp commented. "The work-rate, the determination, the speed."

"He's been on our radar since Rafa's days," Barry Hunter responded.

They were watching footage of the 2017 Africa Cup of Nations. The Pharaohs were on their run to the finals.

"My God! What footwork!" Klopp exclaimed as Mo skipped through Burkina Faso's midfield. "How does he keep it up? Ninety percent humidity, yes?"

"Not the skinny little toe-rag he once was, that's for sure," Hunter said.

"Goal!" Klopp breathed, as Mo buried the Pharaoh's equalizer. He was quiet for a minute.

"Talk to his agent. Is there any way he would consider leaving Roma?"

"What do you think, Maggi?"

It was the end of his second successful season at Roma. Mo was dancing his three-year-old daughter, Makka, around the apartment. The date sweets for breaking the Ramadan fast were ready on the table.

Liverpool's offer had been on the table for a month. Mo liked what Jurgen Klopp said about the team's aspirations; and what he believed Mo offered them. But he hesitated. Luciano Spaletti was good for him. It seemed disloyal to leave so soon after winning a permanent contract here.

Maggi looked up from the bio-technology paper she was reading online.

"Liverpool was your favorite team."

"But another move? Is it good for the girl? For you? We're happy here."

"True, but there is a strong community in England. Besides, it's twice the pay, so twice the charity you can give. You could be a role model over all the world, not just Italy. Not just Egypt. Think of what that means.

"But England is so cold!"

Maggi laughed out loud. "If that is your only reason, then we must go!"

The clock ticked past the minute of sunset. Ramadan was over. Mo lifted a date from the table and popped it into Makka's mouth.

He knew Maggi was right. He thought the same himself. He hoped Spaletti would understand.

Jurgen Klopp smiled broadly as his latest recruit trotted onto Liverpool's Melwood Drive training grounds. Mo smiled back. His heart was pumping. It was his first session with his new team, and he wanted to make a good impression. Roberto Firminio and Sadio Mané came up and shook his hand.

"Nice to meet you, Salah!" Sadio quipped. "Let's make it too hot for our opponents!"

Sadio lifted a ball with his boot and lobbed it toward Mo's chest. Mo let it drop onto his left instep and kept the ball leaping up and down as if his feet were a magnet. He side-footed it to Firminio, who didn't let it touch the ground either before sending it back to Sadio. They played keepie-uppie like that for five minutes, the ball fizzing through the air. It was as if they were all one player.

At last, Jurgen Klopp called the whole team to attention.

"New season, new goals," he said, winking at the three. "Lots of them! We're going to entertain, and win. No-one will out-create us. We will never let any team rest on their ball, no matter who."

He said a few more words, explaining some new ideas, then set everyone to work. Mo listened like a terrier. He had a lot to learn: defensive systems, set plays, attacking patterns. At least the up-tempo, aggressive style should come easily. Jurgen Klopp shouted encouragement as the unfamiliar ways began to sink in.

At the end of the session, Jurgen ran up to Mo and embraced him warmly. "Great work, Mo. There were teething troubles, but you learn fast."

CHAPTER TWENTY-THREE

The Year of Miracles

Two days later, Mo was on the team bus as it drew into Wigan Athletic's DW ground for the second preseason friendly of the 2017/18 campaign.

A few thousand fans had made the short journey northeast from Merseyside. Jurgen Klopp's final words of encouragement rang in Mo's ears as Roberto Firminio side-footed the kick-off in Mo's direction.

It was a competitive game, despite the preseason atmosphere. Although they were two leagues below Liverpool, Wigan scored first, through winger Alex Gilbey. Mo worked hard, his runs from deep and deft touches earning the fans appreciation.

As the clock ticked red for half-time, Phillippe Coutinho hustled and won the ball just inside Wigan's half. He sent a quick pass to Firminio, who darted into the Wigan penalty area and squared it past Wigan's keeper to Mo. It was the simplest of finishes. The first of many. And it felt good. It felt like home.

Mo placed the ball on the penalty spot, breathed in calmly, and took a dozen paces back. In Alexandria's Borg el-Arab stadium, forty thousand Egyptians held their breath. Around the TV in homes and cafés throughout the country, hearts were in mouths.

It was the last minute of the Pharaohs' final World Cup qualification game, against Congo. With a victory, Egypt would go to their first World Cup Finals in thirty years. It was one-all. Mo having supplied Egypt's only goal.

As he waited for the referee's whistle, Mo remembered Mahmoud Fayez, the Pharaoh's assistant manager, giving him the responsibility at their last training session. And he remembered Hamdi Noor, from all those years ago at El Mokawloon.

Practice. Practice. Practice.

He'd grooved the place kick once again last night, over and over. No matter what hung on it, Mo knew his body wouldn't let him down.

The whistle went.

He ran forward.

Shot.

As the ball made the side-netting balloon outward, delirium swept the team, the stands, and the waiting millions across the country.

They were going to Russia! Egypt were going to the World Cup finals!

Back in Anfield, Mo hadn't imagined being taken to the fans' hearts so quickly. They hadn't even reached the end of the year, and his name echoed round the Kop loudly. He was loved here and he was grateful. And he thanked Klopp for unleashing the striker in him. The goals came pouring. Almost as many as one a game, the fastest in Liverpool's history to reach twenty in a season. Calm finishes like the one against Wigan; fabulous long-range strikes; and virtuoso zingers in the penalty area.

For the fans and the club, it meant Liverpool were going places. Riding high in the Premier League, and through to the knock-out stages of the Champions League.

For the last home game of the year, against Leicester City, Mo wanted to do something special.

It began badly. Jamie Vardy putting the visitors in front almost as soon as the game started. Then, in the fifty-second minute, Mo collected a through-ball from Sadio Mané, raced into the box, and side-footed it into the middle of the net. Twenty minutes later, he was at it again. James Milner played him in, and with the Leicester defense like piranhas around him, Mo wove the ball round three players and buried it in the bottom right corner.

He was a magician.

As he walked to the dug-out, ten minutes later, toward a Jurgen Klopp wreathed in smiles, he heard the fans singing.

Mo Salah, Mo Salah, Mo Salah
Running down the wing
Mo Salah-la-la-la-la-ahh
He's the Egyptian King.

Mané, his partner in crime, salaamed in front of him.

In the café in Nagrig and in cafés across Egypt and everywhere in the Middle East they picked it up.

"What a man your son is!" Mayor Shetiah exclaimed. Salah Ghaly just bowed his head in thanks. It was unbelievable.

Melee in the Porto penalty area. James Milner's curling shot cannoned off the far post and up off Mo's feet. He chested it down, flicked it over the Porto keeper's onrush, headed it forward, then toed it expertly home with his trusty left foot.

Two-nil now to Liverpool, as they pulled clear in their away Champions League quarter final. Mo's thirtieth goal of the season. Only one other player in the history of the game had got there so fast.

As the ball hit the net, the fans exploded into yet another Mo Salah chant, pints bobbing up and down as they celebrated in the stands.

Mo Salah-la-la-la-la

Mo Salah-la-la-la-la

If he's good enough for you

He's good enough for me

If he scores another few

Then I'll be Muslim, too.

When the game was over, the chant was all over the internet.

Maggi embraced him as he came through the door of their Liverpool home and Makka ran up.

Mo couldn't help laughing with joy.

After all the struggles, it was everything he dreamed. Bringing happiness, bringing unity, not just to Egyptians, Arabs, and Muslims. But to everyone.

Light

Premier League Player of the Year. Golden Boot. But what mattered most was the people.

Mo sat in the blue-lighted ambulance as it sped through the Kiev streets. After the waves of pain and despair he'd felt in the stadium, he was calm. His arm was strapped, still uncomfortable if he tried to move it, but no longer in agony. Maggi sat at his side, with Makka. They'd hurried from their executive box as soon as he was led off the pitch. Makka's soulful eyes rested on his face.

"God will look after you, Daddy," she said.

He squeezed her hand.

"Look!" Maggi held up his tablet.

His dad had been the first, but messages of support now flooded his Facebook page, his Twitter feed, Instagram, phone, and email. Famous players he'd never even met and colleagues. Spalletti of course and Mourinho. The Egyptian President. But most of all, ordinary fans.

Hundreds, thousands of people, wishing him well in Arabic, Italian, German, English, and tongues he couldn't read, from all across the world.

He closed his eyes, the emotion of it overwhelming him.

"Mr. Salah?"

The paramedic's accented English broke in. "We're at the hospital."

Andrew Massey, Anfield's Head of Medical Services, offered Mo his arm. They were going to X-ray the shoulder to check it was no more than a dislocation. Just a precaution.

Mo pushed himself to his feet and clambered carefully out of the ambulance. A wheeled canvas chair awaited him. It was absurd, but he took it with good grace. They trundled him through the big double doors of the hospital entrance, where blue-uniformed medics ushered him past a half-full waiting room.

There was a TV screen, tuned to the match.

One-one, but Real Madrid had the ball and were flooding upfield.

Liverpool could still do it.

"Hey, Mo Salah!" One of the patients in the waiting room called out excitedly in a drunken Scouse accent. He wore a red shirt and had a bandage round his head. "Shame about the shoulder, mate. Good luck!"

Mo gave the man a thumbs up as he disappeared down the corridor.

The X-ray took less than a minute and Dr. Massey soon came through with the file.

"Your shoulder is dislocated, Mo, that's all," he said.

"How soon can I play?"

Just like when he was a youngster, it was the only thing on his mind.

"Tricky," Massey replied. "Ideally, you don't want to put pressure on that joint for a couple of months. It'll be vulnerable. You'll have to take care, Mo. It's unlikely you'll be a hundred percent for Russia."

"But I *can* play?"

Cautiously, Massey nodded. "Hopefully."

Mo heaved a sigh.

He would be humble, and he would fight. For Nagrig. For Egypt. For all the Liverpool fans. Maybe he wouldn't make it for every game in Russia, but he would fight. Maybe Egypt wouldn't do so well, but he would still fight.

Never stop dreaming. Never stop believing.

He remembered his own words accepting CAF's Player of the Year award. He had never stopped dreaming, or believing. He wouldn't do so now.

He lifted his tablet. The latest messages flashed.

Yalla, Salah.

Whatever happens, we are behind you.

Long live the Egyptian King.

There was always light in the end of the tunnel. He looked at his wife and daughter and smiled.

CPSIA information can be obtained
at www.ICGtesting.com
Printed in the USA
BVHW080952101119
563377BV00002B/239/P